Flags and Seals

ERINN BANTING

WEIGL PUBLISHERS INC.

Project Coordinator
Tina Schwartzenberger

Design
Janine Vangool

Layout
Bryan Pezzi

Copy Editor
Heather Kissock

Photo Research
Wendy Cosh

Published by Weigl Publishers Inc.
350 5th Avenue, Suite 3304
New York, NY USA 10118-0069
Web site: www.weigl.com

Library of Congress Cataloging-in-Publication Data

Banting, Erinn.
  Flags and seals / Erinn Banting.
     v. cm.
Includes index.
Contents: The flag of the United States -- The great seal of the United States -- The presidential flag and seal -- Flags of the Civil War -- Interesting state flags -- Important state seals -- Map of state flags and seals -- Chart of America's state flags and seals.
  ISBN 1-59036-130-X (library bound : alk. paper)
  1. Flags--United States--Juvenile literature. 2. Flags--United States--States--History--Juvenile literature. 3. Flags--Confederate States of America--Juvenile literature. 4. United States--Seal--Juvenile literature. 5. Emblems, National--United States--Juvenile literature. 6. Emblems, State--United States--Juvenile literature. [1. Flags--United States. 2. Flags--United States--States--History. 3. Flags--Confederate States of America. 4. United States--Seal. 5. Emblems, National. 6. Emblems, State.] I. Title.
  CR113.B36 2004
  929.9'2'0973--dc21

                                                    2003005028

Printed in the United States of America
1 2 3 4 5 6 7 8 9 0   07 06 05 04 03

Contents

Introduction

Flags and seals are important symbols to the United States. A symbol is an item that stands for something else. Flags fly outside buildings, schools, and people's homes. Seals are used to

The American flag is often called the Stars and Stripes or the Red, White, and Blue.

authenticate important documents. The country and the individual states each have their own flags and seals. Many special government offices and cities have their own flags and seals, too.

All federal government buildings, including the U.S. Capitol, proudly fly the American Flag. Historic flags are displayed when a new president takes the oath of office.

Flags and seals represent the people, history, and culture of the United States. People proudly display these symbols because they represent **ideals** such as freedom, equality, and justice. Among the best-known flags and seals are the flag of the United States, the Great Seal of the United States, the Presidential Flag and Seal, and the flags of the **Civil War**.

Each of the 50 states has a unique seal. The state seal of New York features the state's official coat of arms encircled by the words "The Great Seal of the State of New York."

The American Flag

The United States's flag is the country's best-known symbol. The flag has thirteen horizontal stripes that alternate red and white. A blue rectangle in the upper left corner features fifty white stars. The stripes represent the original thirteen **colonies** of the United States. The stars represent each of the country's states.

The flag of the United States has changed twenty-seven times since 1776. The Stars and Stripes, the first national flag, had thirteen alternating red and white stripes. A blue square featured a circle of thirteen white stars. In 1795, two new stars and stripes were added to this flag. These additions represented Kentucky and Vermont, the two new states that had joined the **Union**. The stars were arranged in five rows, and the flag came to be known as the Star-Spangled Banner.

By 1818, more new states had joined the Union, and the flag changed again. The design returned to thirteen stripes. The number of stars was changed to reflect every new state in the Union. After 1816, new stars were added to the Star-Spangled Banner every 4th of July, or Independence Day. The fiftieth star was added in 1960, when Hawai'i became a state.

The colors of the American flag are symbolic. White stands for purity and innocence. Red represents strength and heroism. Blue stands for justice.

★ **Historians** disagree about who designed the original Stars and Stripes. For many years, people believed it was Betsy Ross, a seamstress from Philadelphia. Other historians believe the flag was designed by Francis Hopkinson, a politician and writer who signed the **Declaration of Independence**.

★ Mary Pickersgill, a flag maker from Baltimore, made a 1,260-square-foot Star-Spangled Banner. In 1814, Francis Scott Key, a lawyer from Maryland, saw the flag and was inspired to write the national anthem.

★ Rules govern how the American flag should be displayed and flown. When the flag is displayed horizontally or vertically against a wall, the blue field containing the stars should be to the observer's left.

The Great Seal

The Great Seal of the United States was designed after the United States declared independence from England. In 1776, Benjamin Franklin, John Adams, and Thomas Jefferson formed a committee to design a seal for the new country. It took six years, two more committees, and the work of fourteen men before the seal was completed in 1782.

On the seal is an eagle with its wings spread wide apart. The eagle holds thirteen arrows that represent war in its left claw. An olive branch in its right claw represents peace. On the eagle's chest is a shield with thirteen stripes. The thirteen stripes symbolize how the original thirteen colonies of the United States joined to form one country.

Above the thirteen stripes is a blue field called the Chief. The Chief represents all of the different branches of the United States government. Its position on the shield shows that the Chief depends on the union and strength of the states. It also means that the Chief keeps the states united, much in the way that government branches serve the country.

★ The reverse side of the Great Seal appears on the back side of the one dollar bill. It has never been used to authenticate documents.

★ The stripes of the shield on the United States seal are opposite to those on the United States flag. The Great Seal has six red and seven white stripes, while the Star-Spangled Banner has seven red and six white stripes.

★ In 1782, the United States chose the bald eagle as its national bird.

★ The bald eagle holds a banner that reads *E Pluribus Unum*, which is Latin for "One Out of Many." This motto indicates that the United States is a country created by many people joining together as one.

The design of the Great Seal serves to remind Americans of the people who fought for liberty and freedom.

Presidential Flag and Seal

A special flag and seal have been designed for the president of the United States. The flag and seal are similar to the Great Seal of the United States. Both have an eagle clutching arrows in one claw and an olive branch in the other against a blue background. Fifty white stars circle the eagle on the Presidential Seal. The words "Seal of the President of the United States" appear in the outer circle of the seal.

Only the front of the Presidential Seal is stamped on documents.

The design of the flag and seal has changed many times. President Harry S. Truman, the thirty-third president of the United States, wanted the Presidential Flag and Seal to focus on peace, not war. In 1945, he changed the direction the eagle's head faced on the Great Seal, the Presidential Flag, and Presidential Seal. Today, the eagle's head faces the olive branch instead of the arrows, which stands for peace. Also, before 1945, the Presidential Flag had four white stars—one in each corner of the flag. President Truman changed this design so that a circle of fifty white stars, one for each state, surrounds the eagle.

★ The current version of the Presidential Flag was first raised on October 27, 1945, aboard the aircraft carrier *USS Franklin D. Roosevelt.*

★ The first **die** of the Presidential Seal was cut in 1782. The die was used until April 24, 1841. It is on display at the National Archives today. Seven dies have been cut since 1841.

★ The Presidential Seal appears on the buttons of army and air force uniforms of the United States.

Flags of the Civil War

Many flags and seals remind Americans about different periods in their country's history. The northern and southern states fought against each other in the Civil War, which lasted from 1861 to 1865. Slavery was one of the main causes of this war. Many southern landowners forced people to work as slaves on their **plantations**. During the war, several southern states separated and formed the **Confederacy**. The Confederacy created its own flag. During the war, it changed the design of its flag three times. The states of the Union continued to use the Star-Spangled Banner and national seal.

The Stars and Bars was officially adopted as the Confederate national flag on March 4, 1861.

The first Confederate national flag is known as the Stars and Bars. The Confederacy used this flag from March 1861 to May 1863. The flag has one white stripe between red stripes and a field of stars on a blue background. The Confederate national flag contained 13 stars, one for each of the Confederate states. The Confederate states were Alabama, Arkansas, Florida, Georgia, Louisiana, Mississippi, North Carolina, South Carolina, Tennessee, Texas, and Virginia. Stars were also added to the flag for Kentucky and Missouri. These states intended to join the Confederacy but never did.

★ The first version of the Confederate flag had 7 stars. The stars represented the first 7 states to separate from the Union: Alabama, Florida, Georgia, Louisiana, Mississippi, South Carolina, and Texas.

★ Letitia Christian Tyler, granddaughter of President John Tyler, raised the Stars and Bars for the first time.

★ The Confederate national flag created confusion on the battlefield because it looked similar to the Union flag.

★ The Civil War ended in 1865. All states decided to remain part of the union. The end of the war also brought the end of slavery.

Interesting State Flags

Not all flags are national symbols. State flags represent the land and people of the different states. Many stories explain the creation of different state flags.

★ Georgia State Flag

Debate about changing the design of Georgia's flag lasted more than fifteen years. Georgia's flag originally included the Confederate Battle Flag. The Confederate Battle Flag is a **controversial** symbol. It is a reminder of slavery and has been associated with **racist** groups. The design was officially changed on January 31, 2001. The flag now shows the state seal above a gold banner. The banner features the United States flag and the three flags that Georgia has used in the past.

★ Alaska State Flag

In 1927, a 13-year-old Native-American student won a contest to design Alaska's state flag. The flag has a blue background which represents the state flower, the forget-me-not. On the flag are eight gold stars. Seven of these stars form a **constellation** called the Big Dipper. The eighth star represents the North Star. The North Star signifies that Alaska is the most northerly state.

★ Texas State Flag

The Texas state flag has one red and one white stripe, and a blue field with one white star. The flag is nicknamed the "Lone Star" because of this single star. Texas is often called the Lone Star State because of its flag.

★ Washington State Flag

Washington's state flag is the only flag that is mainly green. Washington's flag is also the only state flag that bears the image of one of the country's former presidents. A drawing of the first President of the United States, George Washington, is centered on this state flag.

★ Hawai'i State Flag

The flag of Hawai'i has alternating stripes of white, red, and blue. The eight stripes represent the main islands that make up the state. In the upper left corner is the Union Jack, Great Britain's flag. It is represented on the flag because Great Britain often helped defend Hawai'i from invasion and attack before Hawai'i joined the United States.

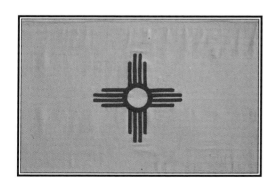

★ New Mexico State Flag

New Mexico's state flag features the Sun with four sets of rays stretching out from it, all in red, on a yellow background. The Sun symbol comes from a Native-American group called the Zia. The rays represent the four directions on a compass, the four seasons, the parts of the day, and stages of life. The rays are all attached to the Sun. They are bound within a circle of life that has no beginning or end.

Important State Seals

State seals are often very elaborate and show the unique people, industries, and characters of each state. There are many stories about the creation of different state seals.

★ Idaho State Seal

Idaho's state seal is the only seal that was designed by a woman, Emma Edwards Green. When the seal was designed in 1890, women in Idaho were not allowed to vote. Emma Edwards Green added a woman to her seal because she believed that women should be allowed to vote.

★ Florida State Seal

Until 1985, the Florida state seal had three mistakes on it. The seal had a Western Plains woman on it, but the first known group of Native Peoples in Florida were Seminole. Steamships like the one on the original seal were never used in Florida, so that was also changed. Finally, the cacao palm tree was changed to a sabal palm, because cacao trees do not grow in the Florida region.

★ Mississippi State Seal

Mississippi has one of the oldest seals in the United States. The design has changed very little since it was first proposed in 1798, before Mississippi became a state. The seal features a bald eagle clutching an olive branch in one claw and arrows in the other. The words "The Great Seal of the State of Mississippi" appear on the outer circle.

★ New York State Seal

Two women on New York's state seal represent liberty and justice. A crown at liberty's foot represents the United States's freedom from England. Liberty also holds a cap similar to those given to Romans who had been released from slavery. Justice wears a blindfold and carries a scale to show the importance of being fair when choosing a punishment.

★ Montana State Seal

Only a few changes have been made to Montana's state seal. Some of the changes have been made without permission. In 1893, the Legislature decided to use the word "state" instead of "territory" on the original seal. When the new seal was **engraved**, the artist, G. R. Metten, changed the design. Changes were made to the way the water flowed, the positioning of the trees, and the shape of the mountains. All of these changes were made without permission from the state government.

★ Illinois State Seal

The state seal of Illinois shows an eagle holding a banner in its mouth. The banner contains the words "State Sovereignty, National Union." In 1867, the Secretary of State proposed that the words be flipped so that the banner read: "National Union, State Sovereignty." The assembly did not accept the Secretary of State's proposal. When the seal was completed, people noticed that the word "sovereignty" was upside down. It was never changed, and the word remains upside down today.

Flags and Seals Everywhere

S tate flags fly all over the United States. Each state also has its own seal. This map shows the flags and seals featured in this book. If your state was not featured, locate your state on the map below. Then, turn the page to learn about your state's flag and seal.

WASHINGTON
5

MONTANA
12

NORTH DAKOTA

IDAHO
8

OREGON

SOUTH DAKOTA

WYOMING

NEBRASKA

NEVADA

UTAH

COLORADO

KANSAS

CALIFORNIA

OKLAHOMA

ARIZONA

NEW MEXICO
7

TEXAS
4

HAWAI'I
6

ALASKA
3

1. Washington, D.C.
2. Georgia
3. Alaska
4. Texas
5. Washington
6. Hawai'i
7. New Mexico
8. Idaho
9. Florida
10. Mississippi
11. New York
12. Montana
13. Illinois

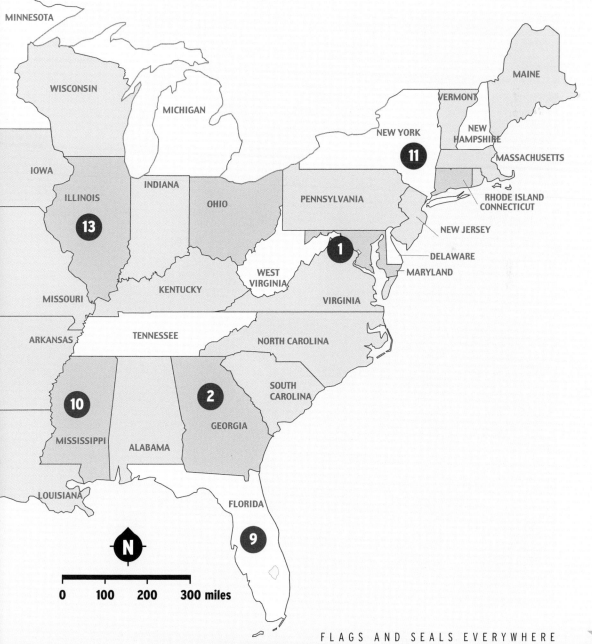

America's State Flags and Seal

Many state flags and seals include national symbols and colors to show a state's national pride. Most states have had more than one flag or seal. This chart lists the year that the flags and seals in use today were adopted.

STATE	STATE FLAG	STATE SEAL
Alabama	Adopted 1895	Adopted 1939
Alaska	Adopted 1927	Adopted 1959
Arizona	Adopted 1917	Adopted 1911
Arkansas	Adopted 1913	Adopted 1907
California	Adopted 1911	Adopted 1849
Colorado	Adopted 1911	Adopted 1861
Connecticut	Adopted 1897	Adopted 1784
Delaware	Adopted 1913	Adopted 1777
Florida	Adopted 1899	Adopted 1868
Georgia	Adopted 2001	Adopted 1798
Hawai'i	Adopted 1959	Adopted 1895
Idaho	Adopted 1907	Adopted 1957
Illinois	Adopted 1915	Adopted 1868
Indiana	Adopted 1917	Adopted 1963
Iowa	Adopted 1921	Adopted 1847
Kansas	Adopted 1927	Adopted 1861
Kentucky	Adopted 1918	Adopted 1792
Louisiana	Adopted 1912	Adopted 1902
Maine	Adopted 1909	Adopted 1820
Maryland	Adopted 1904	Adopted 1959
Massachusetts	Adopted 1915	Adopted 1780
Michigan	Adopted 1911	Adopted 1835

Minnesota	Adopted 1893	Adopted 1861
Mississippi	Adopted 1894	Adopted 1817
Missouri	Adopted 1913	Adopted 1822
Montana	Adopted 1905	Adopted 1893
Nebraska	Adopted 1963	Adopted 1867
Nevada	Adopted 1929	Adopted 1866
New Hampshire	Adopted 1909	Adopted 1931
New Jersey	Adopted 1896	Adopted 1777
New Mexico	Adopted 1925	Adopted 1887
New York	Adopted 1901	Adopted 1882
North Carolina	Adopted 1885	Adopted 1983
North Dakota	Adopted 1911	Adopted 1889
Ohio	Adopted 1902	Adopted 1967
Oklahoma	Adopted 1925	Adopted 1907
Oregon	Adopted 1925	Adopted 1859
Pennsylvania	Adopted 1907	Adopted 1791
Rhode Island	Adopted 1897	Adopted 1875
South Carolina	Adopted 1861	Adopted 1776
South Dakota	Adopted 1963	Adopted 1885
Tennessee	Adopted 1905	Adopted 1987
Texas	Adopted 1845	Adopted 1992
Utah	Adopted 1913	Adopted 1896
Vermont	Adopted 1923	Adopted 1937
Virginia	Adopted 1861	Adopted 1776
Washington	Adopted 1923	Adopted 1889
West Virginia	Adopted 1929	Adopted 1863
Wisconsin	Adopted 1863	Adopted 1851
Wyoming	Adopted 1917	Adopted 1893

Further Research

Every morning, children across the United States recite the Pledge of Allegiance to the United States flag. This ritual reminds the students of the important **principles** of their country. Web sites and books can teach you more about flags and seals.

The stars and stripes of the American Flag are symbols. Stars stand for the heavens. Stripes represent the Sun's rays.

Web Sites

★ For information about the Star-Spangled Banner, visit:
http://americanhistory.si.edu/ssb

★ For information about the national flag, seal, and other symbols, visit:
http://bensguide.gpo.gov/3-5/symbols

★ For more information about state flags and seals, visit:
www.netstate.com/states

★ For information about the flags of the Civil War, visit:
www.nps.gov/gett/gettkidz/flag.htm

Books

★ Knowlton, Laurie L. Red, White, and Blue. Louisiana: Pelican Publishing Company, 2002

★ Munoz Ryan, Pam. The Flag We Love. Watertown: Charlesbridge Publishing, 2000

Create Your Own Seal

Flags and seals remind people of the strength of the nation or state in which they live. If you had your own flag or seal, what would it look like? Try to think of a few of your favorite things that would show other people the kind of person you are. Why are these things special to you? On a piece of paper, draw a picture of your own special flag or seal. Next to the drawing, write what each symbol on your flag or seal means to you.

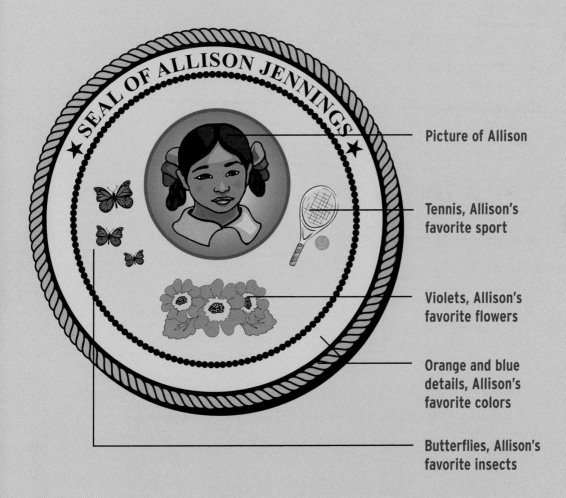

SEAL OF ALLISON JENNINGS

Picture of Allison

Tennis, Allison's favorite sport

Violets, Allison's favorite flowers

Orange and blue details, Allison's favorite colors

Butterflies, Allison's favorite insects

Glossary

★ **authenticate:** to prove something is genuine

★ **Civil War:** a war fought between the North and the South in the United States between 1861 and 1865

★ **colonies:** territories that are ruled by different countries or states

★ **Confederacy:** the southern states that declared themselves separate from the United States in 1860 and 1861

★ **constellation:** a group of stars that form a pattern in the sky

★ **controversial:** causing argument

★ **Declaration of Independence:** a declaration signed on July 4, 1776 that proclaimed the United States' independence from Great Britain

★ **die:** an engraved device that is used to impress a design, similar to a stamp

★ **engraved:** to cut or carve a design

★ **historians:** people who study the past

★ **ideals:** perfect goals

★ **plantations:** large farms

★ **principles:** basic truths, laws, or beliefs

★ **racist:** someone who treats people differently because they believe one race, or large group of people who have similar characteristics, is better than others

★ **Union:** the states that did not separate during the Civil War

Index